T0045251

Who's Best?

Written by
Rob Waring and **Maurice Jamall**

(with contributions by **Julian Thomlinson**)

HEINLE
CENGAGE Learning

Australia • Brazil • Japan • Korea • Mexico • Singapore • Spain • United Kingdom • United States

to draw

to forget

to remember

to tear

art

café

concert

gallery

hair

movie

picture

Kate

Scott

Adib

Yoon-Hee

Gemma

"I can't find my money," says a girl. "Please wait."
She is buying a drink. She opens her bag and looks
for her money. But she cannot find it. Many people
are in The Lagoon café. Everybody is watching her.
"I'm sorry. It's here in my bag. I know," she says.
But she still cannot find it.

A boy speaks to her. "Excuse me," he says. "Here, please take this." He gives her some money.

"But . . . ," says the girl. "I have some money. I just can't find it."

"It's okay," he says. "It's only a drink. It's only a little money."

The girl says, "Thank you. I'll give you the money later."

"It's okay. Are you new here?" he asks.

The girl says, "Yes, I'm new here. I'm Kate."

"Hi. I'm Scott," he says. They both smile.

Scott takes Kate to meet his friends. "Gemma, Yoon-Hee,"
he says. "This is Kate." He smiles at her. Kate sits down
with Scott, Gemma, and Yoon-Hee.
"When did you move to Bayview?" asks Yoon-Hee.
"Yesterday. My family moved here from New York,"
she answers. "Today is my first day here in Bayview."
They talk together for a long time. They become friends.

"Sorry, Kate. I can't stay. I must go now," says Scott.
"But . . . , umm . . . , Kate?" he asks slowly. "What are
you doing on Saturday afternoon?"
Kate says, "I have my art class on Saturday. Why?"
"Oh, I see," he says. "Well, after the class do you
want to see a movie?" he asks. "I can meet you after
your art class."
"Oh yes. Thanks, Scott," she replies. "I'd really like
that. I love movies. Let's meet at 3 o'clock."

"Okay," he says. "See you then. Goodbye."
As Scott leaves, she thinks, "He's really nice. I like him a lot!" He likes her very much, too.
Scott is not looking where he is going. He does not see a boy in a wheelchair.
"Hey! Look out!" says the boy.
Scott does not hear the boy. He's thinking about Kate.

Scott turns and falls over the boy's wheelchair. "Ouch!" says the boy.

Scott is angry with him. "Jimmy! Be careful. Look where you're going!" shouts Scott.

"But, *you* didn't look where you're going!" says Jimmy. "You were looking at that girl."

"You shouldn't be here in your wheelchair," says Scott. "You're dangerous. Go away!"

Jimmy says, "Scott, *you* fell over *me*!"

Kate sees everything. "Why did Scott get angry with Jimmy? Scott wasn't looking," Kate thinks. "Maybe he's not so nice."
Yoon-Hee talks to Kate. "Wow! Scott asked you to go to a movie, Kate!" she says excitedly.
"You're so lucky," says Gemma. "Scott's really good looking."
Kate says, "Yes, he's very nice."
"Nice? Nice!!!" says Gemma. "He's the best boy in Bayview!"
"I don't know," says Kate. She is thinking about Scott and Jimmy.

"Oh, Kate!" says Gemma. "All the girls want to go out with Scott!"

"He's really nice and everything," says Kate. "And he's so good looking. But I don't know him very well."

Yoon-Hee asks, "What do you want to know, Kate? All the girls are in love with him."

"Yes. They are, Kate," says Gemma.

"Hmm . . . ," thinks Kate.

On Saturday afternoon, Kate goes to her art class.
"Good afternoon, everybody," says the teacher.
"My name's Mrs. Chen. I'm going to teach you to draw."
Mrs. Chen says, "Let's start with drawing the face.
Find a partner and sit together. Please start."
"Hi," says the boy next to Kate. "Do you want to
work together?"
Kate smiles, "Hi, okay."

"I'm new here," she says.

"Really? I'm new, too. My name's Adib," he says. "I'm from Chicago. Where are you from?"

Kate says, "I'm Kate, I'm from New York. My family came here a week ago."

"Really," says Adib. "The best art galleries are in New York." Kate starts to draw Adib. They talk a lot. They talk about art and artists. Kate likes Adib.

"He knows a lot about art. He's nice and very easy to talk to," she thinks.

Mrs. Chen says, "Show your pictures to your partner, please."
Kate shows her picture to Adib. "Do you like it?" she asks.
"I'm sorry, the hair is strange."
"It's a nice picture," he replies. "That's okay, because my hair's always strange." Adib smiles. He shows Kate his drawing. She looks at it for a long time.
"It's really great," she says. "You're a very good artist, Adib."
"The eyes are very hard to draw," says Adib. "But you have . . . , nice eyes . . . They are easy to draw."

"You can keep the picture, Kate," says Adib. "It's for you."
"Really? Oh, thank you so much, Adib," she says happily.
Adib says, "I really like drawing."
"Me too!" she says.
"Which artists do you like best?" he asks.
Kate says, "I really like Joan Miro and Picasso the most.
And you?"
"I like Van Gogh. Look at this picture," he says. Adib shows
her a book.

"I like the way Van Gogh used strong colors. He's the most interesting artist, I think," he says. Adib knows a lot about art and pictures.

"Yes, he's very interesting," she says.

He says, "Van Gogh tried to say things in his pictures." Adib and Kate talk about art for a long time. They look at many pictures together. Kate is enjoying her art class so much, she forgets about Scott.

It is nearly 5 o'clock. Scott is waiting for Kate. He comes into the art class.

"Kate, what happened?" he says. "We're late for the movie!"

"Hi, Scott," says Kate. "I'm so sorry. I forgot. I was talking with Adib about art." She feels very bad.

"We're late for the movie. It's too late to go now," he says.

Adib says, "Oh, I'm sorry, Kate. I didn't know your plans."

"That's okay, Adib. Look at this picture, Scott. Adib did it. Do you like it?" says Kate.

Scott looks at the picture. Then he looks hard at Adib. "It's not very good, Kate," he says. "You're much more beautiful than this."
"Yes," says Adib. "I'm sorry. I didn't draw her face well."
"I wasn't talking to you," Scott says angrily to Adib.
"Adib's picture is very bad, Kate. I don't like it," says Scott.

Suddenly, Scott takes the picture from Kate. She is very surprised.

"What are you doing, Scott? That's my picture," she says. Scott does not listen. He tears the picture in two.

"I'm sorry, Kate," says Scott. "But that was a bad picture. I can get a really nice one for you."

"Hey, Scott," says Kate. "That was *my* picture! Why did you tear it?" She is angry with Scott.

Later, Scott calls Kate. "I'm sorry about today," he says. "I was wrong. I was angry. I was waiting a long time and I wanted to go to the movie with you."

"I know. I'm sorry," says Kate. "But you *were* wrong to tear my picture."

Scott says, "I thought you liked that boy more than me."

Kate says, "I don't know him well. He's a student in the art class. I met him today."

"Oh?" says Scott. "I'm sorry. Look, Kate, there's a concert by Hot Rock on Saturday night. Can you come?"

"Okay," she says. "I'll see you at about 6 o'clock on Saturday. Bye."

The next Monday, Kate is talking with Yoon-Hee.
"Hi, Kate. Are you going to the concert this Saturday?" asks Yoon-Hee.
"Yes, Scott asked me to go with him," Kate tells her.
"You're so lucky, Kate," says Yoon-Hee. "He's so good looking!"
She says, "Yes, he is. But . . . "
"But what?" asks Yoon-Hee.
"I don't know. I'm not sure about Scott. Yes, he's very good looking, but I don't know him that well," she says slowly. She is thinking about Adib.

Adib sees Kate in the café. "Hello, Kate," says Adib. "Do you remember me? We met on Saturday in art class."

"Yes, of course, Adib. I remember you," says Kate. "I'm sorry about Saturday."

"That's okay. It was fun," says Adib. "I understand." He smiles at her.

"He's quiet and has a nice smile," thinks Kate. "But Scott has a nice smile too, and he's better looking than Adib."

"Kate, what are you doing after the art class next Saturday?" asks Adib.

Kate asks, "Why, Adib?"

"There's an art show at Bayview Art Gallery," says Adib. "It's a show for new artists. Do you want to come?"

"Oh, I *am* sorry, Adib," she says. "But I'm going to a concert with Scott."

"Oh, with Scott . . . I see," says Adib. "That's okay." But Adib's eyes do not look happy.

"I'm sorry too, Adib," she says.

The next Saturday, Scott comes to Kate's house. Kate looks very beautiful.

"You look really beautiful, Kate," says Scott. "Let's go!"

Kate says nothing. She walks to the taxi and looks at Scott. She thinks about Scott, and about Adib. She looks at Scott, and thinks, "He looks nice, but he's not a nice person."

"Thanks," says Kate. "But being good looking, or beautiful is not the only thing."

Later, at the art gallery, Kate meets Adib.
"I'm very happy you're here," says Adib.
Kate says, "Me too, Adib. Me too."
"I want to show you something, Kate. Come with me,"
says Adib.
Adib and Kate walk to a picture. It is a picture of Kate!
"Adib! It's very good. How did you draw it?" asks Kate.
"I remembered your eyes, Kate." Adib smiles.
"I remembered your eyes."